Workshop Models for Family Life Education

Children of Divorce

Marilyn A. Davenport, Patricia L. Gordy, and
Nancy A. Miranda

Families International, Inc.
Milwaukee, Wisconsin

The artwork on the cover and illustrations throughout the book were created by the following participants in children of divorce groups: Erica Armbruster, Crystal Czar, Annie Maré Hughes, Robert Markle, William Markle, Gretchen Melissa Ott, Heidi Kathleen Ott, and Stephanie Ann.

Copyright 1993
Families International, Inc.
Published in association with
Family Service America, Inc.
11700 West Lake Park Drive
Milwaukee, Wisconsin 53224

Library of Congress Cataloging-in-Publication Data

Davenport, Marilyn A.
    Children of divorce / Marilyn A. Davenport, Patricia L. Gordy, and
Nancy A. Miranda.
      p. cm. — (Workshop models for family life education)
   "Published in association with Family Service America"—T.p.
verso.
   Includes bibliographical references.
   ISBN 0-87304-265-4
   1. Children of divorced parents—United States—Counseling of.
2. Group counseling for children.   I. Gordy, Patricia L.
II. Miranda, Nancy A.   III. Title.   IV. Series.
HQ777.5.D38 1992
306.89—dc20   92-35959

Printed in the United States

CONTENTS

PREFACE

Workshop Models for Family Life Education is a series of manuals intended to promote the exploration of new alternatives and the utilization of new options in day-to-day living through programs in family life education.

Basically, family life education (FLE) is a service of planned intervention that applies the dynamic process of group learning to improving the quality of individual and family living. The manuals are in workshop format and offer new approaches to service to families. They are meant to serve as a training mechanism and basic framework for group leaders involved in FLE workshops.

In 1974, the Family Service Association of America (FSAA), now Family Service America, Inc., appointed a National Task Force on Family Life Education, Development, and Enrichment. One of the goals of the task force was to assess the importance and future direction of FLE services within family service agencies. One of the recommendations of its report was to "recognize family life education, development, and enrichment as one of the three major services of the family service agency: family counseling, family life education, and family advocacy."[1] This recommendation was adopted by the association's Board of Directors and has become basic policy.

An interest in FLE is a natural development of Family Service America's role in the strengthening of family life and complementary to the more traditional remedial functions of family agencies. Family Life Education programs can add a new dimension to the services provided by family agencies. They can open an agency to the general population by providing programs that are appropriate for all families and individuals, not only for those at risk. They provide a new arena for service that deals with growth as well as dysfunction. They can encourage agencies to look beyond the therapeutic approach and to take on a new objective for the enrichment and strengthening of family life. For the participants, FLE programs can lead to increased understanding of normal stress, growth of esteem for one's self and others, development of communications skills, improved ability to cope with problem situations, development of problem-solving skills, and maximization of family and individual potential.

This series provides tangible evidence of Family Service America's continuing interest in FLE and of a belief in its future importance for family services. Family Life Education programs, coordinated within a total agency program and viewed as a vital and integral part of the agency, can become key factors in promoting growth and development within all families.

---

1. "Overview of Findings of the FSAA Task Force on Family Life Education, Development, and Enrichment," mimeographed (New York: Family Service Association of America, May 1976), p. 21.

ACKNOWLEDGMENTS

We are indebted to many people for help in supporting our collaborative efforts in writing this book. Through the Family Service America, Inc., network of member agencies, we contacted Jean Strecker, Director of the Families in Transition program at Family and Children's Service of Nashville, Tennessee. She readily lent her advice and background materials. We launched our initial groups with much support from staff and students within the Nazareth Area School District, Nazareth, Pennsylvania. We also received encouragement and ample support from the entire staff and student interns at Family and Counseling Services of the Lehigh Valley in Allentown, Pennsylvania. Ultimately, we are grateful to the children and their families, separated and divorced, who have participated in our groups and taught us about courage in accepting changes in their lives.

Marilyn A. Davenport
Patricia L. Gordy
Nancy A. Miranda

GENERAL INFORMATION

This Family Life Education workshop is directed toward helping children cope with the crisis of divorce and to anticipate further difficulties that they may yet face in connection with their parents' divorce. The workshop's aim is both preventive and curative.

Family and Counseling Services of the Lehigh Valley has offered this group in school settings, day care centers, and at the agency itself. The program consists of eight sessions, each of which should last at least 60 minutes. Ninety-minute sessions, if more time is available, allow greater flexibility for leaders and more time for discussion. If 90-minute sessions are scheduled, we recommend a short break for participants midway through the session.

In general, the material is appropriate for children ages 6 to 12. We recommend that children be grouped with a maximum span of three years between members, in other words, children ages 6 to 8, 9 to 11, and 10 to 12 can be grouped together. The workshop works best for groups numbering approximately six to eight children. In our experience, the time elapsed since the family disruption and the workshop experience is of little consequence. Children in the midst of the crisis can benefit, as can those further along in the process. In one case we encountered, a child whose parents had been divorced for 10 years still struggled with issues stemming from the divorce.

The workshop sessions often include group exercises and activities, because frequently children have feelings and ideas associated with their family situations that are too new or too painful to deal with directly. We have found it helpful to create exercises that allow children to discuss their experiences while maintaining a comfortable psychological and emotional distance from the events. They can be creative and have fun while they identify issues and feelings that need expression and management.

ORGANIZING THE WORKSHOP

When presenting and marketing the group, a letter is sent to parents (see page x) describing the program content and registration process. As part of the registration process, parents' written permission for their child's participation should become a matter of record. Parents should be informed that the group process is an extremely effective way to help children cope with divorce. However, on rare occasions, a child may have difficulty adjusting to the group or may have needs that would be better addressed by individual counseling. In such instances, parents might be asked to withdraw their child from the group and to seek another form of counseling. In addition, the confidential nature of workshop discussions, which is explained and stressed to the children in the group during the first session, should be pointed out to the parents as well.

The parents should also be told that each child will compile the results of group exercises and activities into a book that will be his or hers to keep at the end of the workshop. Group books represent each child's individual experience of divorce and can be used at home to generate discussion, address problems, and, most important, share feelings. If examples from previous groups are available, group books are often helpful tools in explaining the group experience to parents, teachers, and other interested parties.

It is important for workshop leaders involved with children's groups to be aware of state laws regarding the reporting of suspected physical or sexual abuse. In the event that disclosures of abuse are made by children during group sessions, workshop leaders should be prepared to act in accordance with state reporting requirements.

MATERIALS

The following materials are needed for conducting group sessions:

- ✔ Drawing paper, paper plates, file cards, crayons, pencils, and colored markers
- ✔ Chalkboard or newsprint flip chart

Other materials and preparations for individual sessions are outlined in those sessions.

RESOURCES

Several books are extremely helpful in covering various points and issues during the sessions, and the specific use of some of these books is discussed in the individual sessions. These books and other useful publications include:

Berry Berger, *How Does It Feel When Your Parents Get Divorced?* New York: Julian Messner, 1977.

Laurene Krasay Brown and Marc Brown, *Dinosaurs Divorce.* Boston: Little, Brown and Company, 1986.

Joan Fassler, *The Boy with a Problem.* New York: Human Sciences Press, 1971. (Out of print, check your local library for a copy.)

Richard Gardner, *The Boys and Girls Book about Divorce.* New York: Bantam, 1971. (Book is appropriate for children in grades 4 and up.)

Richard Gardner, *The Boys and Girls Book about Divorce* (grade 7 and up). Northvale, NJ: Jason Aronson, 1983.

Meredith Tax, *Families.* Boston: Little, Brown and Company, 1981.

Judith Viorst, *The Tenth Good Thing about Barney.* New York: Atheneum, 1971.

Another tool that can be helpful in stimulating discussion is the videotape. Your local library as well as area video-rental businesses can be a resource for this material. The Center for Divorce Education (P.O. Box 5900, Athens, Ohio 45701) also makes videos available. For instance, the Center distributes a videotape called "Children in the Middle," which illustrates ways that parents involve children in their disputes and suggests how parents and children can deal with the problems this causes. Another video resource is "Do Children Also Divorce?" This tape is distributed by CECOM Hospital, Riviere-des-Prairies, Quebec, Canada. It shows the reactions of children of various ages to their parents' impending divorce.

SAMPLE LETTER TO PARENTS

Dear Parent:

If you have a child who has experienced the separation or divorce of parents, the program described below may be of interest to you.

Each year in the United States, two million children younger than 18 years of age are caught in the middle of a family breakup. Often parents are so involved with their own crises they don't know how to help their children, and even the best parents, because they are a part of the situation, may not be the best "helpers" for their own children.

Research has identified the common problems that children affected by divorce must face and overcome if they are to progress in growth, performance, and future relationships. (Agency or Program Name) has designed a program to help young people ages six through the early adolescent years to deal with the issues of separation and divorce. During the course of eight sessions with a group of young people of similar age, they will tackle the following problems and topics:

- ✔ What is a family, anyway? Is there something strange about mine?
- ✔ How do I really feel about the divorce?
- ✔ Why does it hurt so much? (Loss)
- ✔ What can I do about it? (Accepting, dealing, and living with divorce; evaluating and learning new coping mechanisms)
- ✔ Building self-esteem

Your young person will have the benefit of sharing his or her experience with others in the same situation. It matters little when the divorce occurred, because these issues remain with the child for a long time. We can help him or her understand and deal with the variety of problems and changes that occur when a family breaks up. He or she will also have the opportunity to bring home group material so that you know what is being dealt with and can share in this process.

(Information on fee and registration process)

We hope you will take advantage of this program and look forward to meeting you.

Sincerely,

INTRODUCTION

Each year more than one million families in the United States experience divorce. The children from these families are caught in the emotional, social, and economic whirlwind that accompanies the divorce process.

Parents are often overwhelmed with their own issues regarding divorce and are not always available to help their children cope. Children are then left to struggle with the family breakup on their own. Taking on this additional burden often interferes with their normal developmental process. As children struggle to cope with issues surrounding the divorce, they are left with no time or energy to address their own individual growth and development.

According to Judith Wallerstein, children face six psychological tasks in the process of understanding and coping with their parents' divorce. Wallerstein's six tasks are summarized as follows:[1]

Task I: Acknowledging the Reality of the Marital Rupture
The child or adolescent needs to overcome a desire to deny the family rupture. He or she also needs to turn from the use of fantasy to avoid reality and to avoid facing fears about the distressing situation.

Task II: Disengaging from Parental Conflict and Resuming Customary Pursuits
The child or adolescent needs to separate him- or herself from the parental conflict. This is difficult because the child/adolescent worries about his or her parents, and parents may feel the need to obtain nurturance and support from the child. Also, the child must keep the family crisis from dominating his or her inner world and master whatever anxiety or depression he or she feels in relation to the divorce.

Task III: Resolution of Loss
The child or adolescent needs to mourn the multiple losses caused by divorce. The child also needs to overcome his or her deep sense of rejection, humilia-

tion, unlovability, and powerlessness—feelings that a parent's departure often engenders.

Task IV: Resolving Anger and Self-Blame

Divorce often causes children to feel anger at the parent who initiated the divorce or at both parents for what the child perceives as their self-centeredness or unresponsiveness to the child's wish to keep the family intact. Children are often angry at themselves for once having wished the divorce would happen or for having failed to restore the marriage. Children need to forgive themselves and one or both parents.

Task V: Accepting the Permanence of the Divorce

The child or adolescent needs to accept the permanency of the divorce and to relinquish the fantasy that the family will be reunited.

Task VI: Achieving Realistic Hope Regarding Relationships

The child or adolescent needs to achieve a realistic vision with regard to his or her capacity to give and receive love. This task is usually confronted during adolescence.

This workshop is designed to address the six psychological tasks outlined by Wallerstein. The following table summarizes which sessions address each task:

Task	Session
I	1, 2
II	2, 5, 7, 8
II	3
IV	4, 5, 6
V	2, 4, 6
VI	1, 6, 7, 8

Wallerstein's longitudinal studies have shown that the overall effects of the multiple losses and stresses of divorce can linger far into adulthood for children who feel overwhelmed by the changes in their families. Regardless of the age of the child at the time of divorce, the child will eventually face the six tasks in the course of his or her development.[2] The children of today will be marital partners and parents tomorrow. They will need tools and guidance as they try to form meaningful relationships and intimacy in their evolving family experiences.

The overall objectives of this workshop are to provide discussion opportunities and exercises that enhance children's individuation and self-esteem. The sessions are designed to help children develop problem-solving skills, coping mechanisms, and increased self-awareness as well as to help alleviate the strong feelings of anger, guilt, and sadness engendered by the family crisis of divorce. Each session attempts to deal directly with the common problems and adjustments that children of divorce face.

We have incorporated into the workshop several basic themes:

✔ All families are important, no matter what their composition or residence.

✔ Children often experience a range of common feelings and reactions to the losses of separation and divorce, including anger, guilt, fear, and sadness.

✔ Each new problem encountered by a child implies a new solution to be discovered.

✔ Children should find activities and interests to help them engage in meaningful activity while they adjust to changes in their families.

✔ Children should seek out trusted individuals with whom to talk about their concerns or problems.

✔ Each child has positive traits, often representing characteristics or teachings of both parents, which are strengths derived from the family.

We hope that the children in your group will learn skills that help them overcome many of the difficulties they encounter in connection with their parents' divorce. What they learn now can help them direct their own futures and enhance their future relationships.

NOTES

1. Judith S. Wallerstein, "Children of Divorce: The Psychological Tasks of the Child," *American Journal of Orthopsychiatry,* 53 (April 1983): 230–243.

2. Judith S. Wallerstein, *Second Chances* (New York: Ticknor and Fields, 1989).

Session 1

THE FAMILY

OBJECTIVES

✔ To orient members to the group's structure, rules, content, goals, and purposes
✔ To help group members get acquainted with each other and with the leader(s)
✔ To introduce the concept of variations in family structure and composition
✔ To help group members define "family" in general and their own in particular
✔ To help children identify the effects that separation and divorce have had on their family
✔ To facilitate self-disclosure through both verbal and nonverbal modes of communication

MATERIALS

✔ Poster board or large sheets of paper on which to write group rules
✔ Paper and crayons or pencils for drawing
✔ Chalkboard, flip chart, or large sheets of paper for leader to write on

BRIEF OUTLINE

I. Introduction to Group
II. Group Rules
III. Get-Acquainted Activity
IV. Mini-Lecture: Families
V. Family-Picture Activity
VI. Summary of Session
VII. Anticipating the Next Session

I. INTRODUCTION TO GROUP

A. *Greetings*
As group members enter the room, greet them and show them
where they are to sit. A circular table works especially well with
children, because they all face one another and no one is put at
the head of the table.

B. *Introduce Leader(s)*
Introduce yourself and any co-leader(s) to the group. Explain to
the children what organization or group you represent. Many sessions are held in "host" settings, such as schools, churches, or
day-care centers, and the children need to understand that the
group is separate from the host setting and its programs. Tell the
group the name by which you would like to be called.

C. *Purpose of Group*
Explain the purpose and basic goals of the group. The following
introduction has been helpful for groups of young children, but
can be tailored to fit the age of the children you are serving:

"I'm delighted that you've decided to join our special support
group. Everyone in the group has experienced either a separation
or a divorce in his or her family. I know that having parents who
live in separate homes can bring about a lot of changes in your
life. Sometimes it is really confusing to be a member of a family
that changes. Many children have said that it helps to talk to other
children close to their age who have been through the same experiences. When persons talk to others about things that bother them
or difficult problems, very often these problems seem to get small-
er. That's what we hope will happen in this group.

"We've designed this special support group so that each of you
will have a comfortable place to talk about what it has been like
for you to go through a family separation or divorce. I hope you
will be able to see that you are not alone. I want you to hear what

other children are saying about divorce. Perhaps you have had things happen to you that are just like what happened to someone else in the group. Some of you may be in special situations. I hope that, as you share your thoughts and feelings about your family, you can learn something that will help you."

D. *Structure of the Group*
Explain where the group will meet, how long sessions will last, and how many meetings will be held. Stress that it is important for the group members to come to every meeting so that they can get the most help from the group. Ask if anyone has a question about the group at this point.

II. GROUP RULES

It may be helpful to introduce the idea of structure to the group and set some limits on behavior by a general discussion of group rules. The following material, tailored to the age of the children, can accomplish this early in the group. Write the basic rules on poster board and bring them to each session. Display the rules during the first few sessions and refer to them when needed to maintain order and focus.

"Have any of you ever been in a discussion group before? Have any of you been in other groups, like activity groups such as scouts or 4H? Chances are you know that all groups have special rules to make sure everyone feels at home in the group and each person has a chance to talk. Here are the basic rules for our group:

A. *"Talk one at a time so everyone can be heard.*
If several of you want to talk at the same time, raise your hand and I'll call on you. Let the speaker say all he or she wants to say without interrupting. I'll see to it that everyone gets a turn to talk.

B. *"If you don't feel like talking, you can pass and just listen.*
No one will be forced to talk, but I hope everyone will share thoughts and feelings, because everyone has important things to say.

C. *"Everyone's feelings will be respected.*
No one should laugh or tease the person who is talking. You
wouldn't want the same thing done to you. I hope that you'll listen
carefully to the person who is speaking. You can do this by look-
ing at the speaker and not making noises while someone is talking. Stay in your seat when the group is having discussion time
and try to pay attention. This helps the group work for everyone.

D. *"What is said in the group is private.*
Everyone should respect the basic rules of the group and not report
to people outside the group the private things that are said by others
in the group meetings. You can feel free to talk about your **own** feelings with your parents, teachers, counselors, or good friends or to
tell others about the activities that we do together in our meetings.
Your parents already know about the rule for keeping the things
other children say private because I've talked with them about it.

"Let me give you an example of this rule: It's O.K. to tell someone
whom you trust that you feel sad when your dad doesn't visit or
when your parents fight. It's O.K. to tell someone that you learned
others feel sad when these things happen to them, too. But it's **not**
O.K. to tell someone else that 'Susie' cries and feels sad when her
dad doesn't visit or her parents fight. Does everyone understand
this rule? Have any of you heard of this rule, called the rule of
confidentiality, before? Have you ever told anyone something private or a secret and found out later that they told this to others?
How did that make you feel? We'll be talking a lot in this group
about how important it is to be able to trust people. One of the
ways we need to trust each other, and for you to learn to trust me,
is to keep the rule of confidentiality."

III. GET-ACQUAINTED ACTIVITY

In order to ease the process of children introducing themselves to the
group and break up didactic material with activity-oriented tasks, we
have found that a drawing exercise at this point is helpful. In addition,

this activity links the children's identity with a positive rather than negative characteristic or situation and begins the group on an optimistic note. Introduce the activity in the following manner:

"One way for us to get to know one another better and to help us remember everyone's name is to have you draw a picture of a favorite activity that you enjoy. Activities and hobbies are important ways to help each of us manage the changes that come into our lives with divorce. Would each of you please take a sheet of paper and crayons or pencils and draw a picture of something you enjoy doing in your free time? Don't put your name on the picture. We'll be using these pictures to learn names of group members. It can be any picture that will help us think about what you like to do."

Allow about five minutes for the group to complete this task.

A. Ask each child to hold up his or her picture to show to the group, state his or her name, and explain what the picture portrays. You might like to see if the group can guess the activity before the

child reveals it. Make sure that each child participates, even if he or she has not had enough time to complete the picture.

B. Now collect all the pictures and scramble them. Select a picture to show and ask the group if they can recall whose picture it is and what the person enjoys doing. If a respondent can identify the activity but not the child's name, ask for help from the group. Allow five minutes for this activity.

C. Tell the group that future meetings will start with this exercise to help everyone learn the others' names. Also tell the group that you will keep these pictures for them and return them at the end of the group, so they will all have them to put in their group books.

D. Review for the group the range of activities shared by members. Accent similarities as well as differences. You may want to ask how many others enjoy the activity depicted in any particular picture. These interchanges begin the process of group identity, cohesion, and interaction.

E. *Preview of Future Group Activities*
By sharing tentative plans for future group activities with the children at this time, some anxieties are lessened and the children are better prepared for the program. Tell the children that over the course of the group, they will be participating in the following activities:

Activity pictures, family pictures, reading special books together, making time lines to mark special events in their lives, worksheets on feelings, questionnaires especially for children of divorce, win–lose–draw games, role playing skits and situations, original group stories, writing an advice column for children of divorce, activity-pie exercise, and a pie-plate-faces exercise about feelings.

F. *Group Book about Divorce*
Explain to the children that each of the drawing or writing projects they do will be collected and become part of their very

own "Book about Divorce" that they will be able to take home with them at the end of the group. Their book will be a special record of their group experience and the things that they learned about dealing with separation and divorce in their families. If you have access to sample books from previous groups, this is a good time to share those examples with the current group.

Depending on the resources available to the leader, the books can be compiled in a number of ways. The materials can be stapled together, placed in a presentation folder, or bound with yarn. As an additional, optional group activity, the children can create their own book covers during the last session.

IV. MINI-LECTURE: FAMILIES

Meredith Tax's book *Families*[1] and similar resources contain a wealth of information to draw on in discussing the topic of families. A mini-lecture such as the following challenges the group members to expand their ideas about families, to define what a family is, and to identify their own unique family.

"Although each member of this group is different from every other member, you all have one special place in common. Each of you belongs to a family. You received your name and all the special characteristics of how you look and how you act from your family. Families are very important to all of us. Families include both people we love and people with whom we live. Many children today have people whom they love and people with whom they live in two or more separate houses. Even when your parents don't live together anymore, they are still a part of your family.

"Do you know how many American families go through separation and divorce each year? One million American families go through divorce every year and live in separate homes. One million families is a lot of people and they have all gone through an experience similar to yours. In fact, half of all American children will experience separation and divorce in their family before they are 18 years of age. What I'm saying is that you're not alone in what is happening to your family.

"Think about your classmates in school. About one-third to one-half of them are probably from divorced families. You're not alone. You probably know classmates and friends whose parents are divorced. I'll bet there are others you're not aware of. Take a look at this group. Each of you knows what it's like to go through the changes that divorce brings about in a family. Did you know this about each other before you joined this group?

"We'll spend part of our time today talking about how important our families are. Even if the members of your family have been going through some changes, it's important for you to remember that you're still connected to one another as family. When you look around the world of nature, you see animals have a mother and father. Some animal groups have one mother, one father, and their babies—like cats, dogs, and birds. Does anyone know of an animal for which 'family' means one father, several different mothers, and hundreds of babies? A single rooster in a barnyard will often mate with several hens and produce lots and lots of babies. Can anyone think of another animal family that has one mother, several fathers, and lots of babies? In the bee world, there is a single queen bee who is the mother for the hive, several father bees, and hundreds of baby bees. Perhaps you can think of other animals that have special family patterns.

"People live in a variety of family patterns, too. Today we'll highlight all the different types of families represented by our group. Some children live with one parent and visit the other parent. Some children live with one parent and never see their other parent. Or you can live with grandparents, foster parents, aunts, uncles, godparents, and so forth. Sometimes a child's parents get divorced and one parent marries someone else. That child lives with one biological parent, a new stepfather or stepmother, and maybe some stepbrothers or stepsisters.

That kind of family is called a **blended** family. No matter what your family pattern is, your family is important.

"Because we can't really tell what a family is only by who lives together, we have to have another way to decide what the meaning of the word 'family' is. We see families can take many shapes, be large or small, be under one roof or several. Maybe none of that is as important as what makes a family so special to each of us, and maybe that's what a family really is: People who love and care about one another, no matter what their living situation is. *A family can be anyone you live with or anyone you love."*

V. FAMILY-PICTURE ACTIVITY

A. "Now that we know more about what a family is—anyone you live with or anyone you love—we have a special activity for you to do to help you discover what kind of a family you have. Please take a sheet of paper, pencils, and crayons and draw a picture of your family. Put in your picture the people who you feel are a part of your family— anyone you live with or anyone you love. So we can get to know your family better, write the person's name beside his or her picture." Allow five to ten minutes for this activity.

B. When the children have finished their pictures, ask each child to introduce his or her family to the group by using the picture. Have the child identify each person in the picture by name and by relationship to the child.

C. As the children discuss their pictures, use a blackboard or newsprint flip chart to list all of the different types of families that are represented by the group, such as single-parent mother, single-parent father, blended family, foster family, etc. Explain to the group what you are doing as you go through this process. When the exercise is complete, review the list with the group and comment on how many different types of families the children live in—different

people, perhaps different houses, but all are alike in one important way: Your family is anyone you live with and anyone you love.

D. Collect all the pictures and remind the children that you will return these special pictures at the end of the group so that they can put them in their group books.

VI. SUMMARY OF SESSION

Review for the group the key points of this session:

A. You are not alone in your experience of divorce. The group can be a safe place to talk about your particular experience and hear from others what their experience is like.

B. Group rules help to make the group work better and more fun for everyone. Confidentiality is expected from all group members.

C. Enjoyable hobbies and activities help to make us feel better while our families go through changes. Our group will do a lot of different activities, too. These activities will help you to express your own thoughts and feelings about divorce.

D. Each of you will be putting together a special book for you to take home when the group is done.

E. Families are important. There are many different kinds, but we all belong to a family made up of anyone we live with and anyone we love.

VII. ANTICIPATING THE NEXT SESSION

Tell the group that next week they will talk about feelings—what they are and what to do with them.

NOTE

1. Meredith Tax, *Families* (Boston: Little, Brown and Co., 1981).

Session 2
FEELINGS

OBJECTIVES

✔ To help children understand what a feeling is
✔ To help children recognize and name their feelings
✔ To help children understand that everyone has
  both good and bad feelings
✔ To provide a safe atmosphere in which children can express
  their feelings about divorce

MATERIALS

✔ White construction paper or paper plates on which to
  draw faces illustrating feelings
✔ If working with older children, file cards on which to write the
  names of feelings
✔ Paper, crayons, pencils, or colored markers for drawing

BRIEF OUTLINE

   I. Preparation for Session
  II. Opening the Session
 III. Discussion of Feelings
 IV. Mini-Lecture: Feelings
  V. Feelings Activity and Discussion
 VI. Summary of Session
VII. Anticipating the Next Session

I. PREPARATION FOR SESSION

A. If working with children approximately 4 to 8 years of age, follow step 1. If working with children approximately 9 to 12 years of age, follow step 2.

Step 1: Use white construction paper or white paper plates and colored markers to make faces. Draw faces simply and clearly to illustrate feelings of happiness, sadness, fear, and anger. You may choose to include other emotions as well.

Step 2: Cut white construction paper into two-by-three-inch rectangles to make cards or use the back of three-by-five-inch file cards. On these cards, write the names of the following feelings: anger, hurt, fear, hate, worry, shame, love, guilt, sadness, happiness, sympathy, frustration, confusion, excitement, and disappointment. You may choose to include others.

B. Have drawing paper and crayons or colored markers available for the children.

II. OPENING THE SESSION

Tell group members that you are going to see how well they remember one another from the previous session. Hold up the pictures that were made during the get-acquainted activity in Session 1. As you hold up each picture, ask, "Whose picture is this, and what does this person enjoy doing?" Make sure each child is identified. If the group members cannot remember someone's name, give them hints to help or identify the child for them.

Next, point to the poster of group rules and remind members that everyone must always follow group rules.

Ask if the children have any questions or comments about last week's session on different kinds of families.

III. DISCUSSION OF FEELINGS

Introduce the concept of feelings by asking the group:

A. What is a feeling?

B. Who has feelings?

C. Where do feelings come from?

IV. MINI-LECTURE: FEELINGS

"All human beings have feelings. Feelings can also be called emotions or sensations. It's very difficult to describe what a feeling is until you put a name to it—like happy, angry, sad, and so on. Those are just a few examples of feelings, and we all have hundreds of different kinds of feelings.

"Some feelings we really like to have—happiness, for example. Some we never want to have, like sadness. All of our feelings, though, tell us about ourselves and what is going on in our world. It is important for us to 'feel' or recognize all of our feelings. Can you imagine never feeling happy, excited, or proud? When you have these feelings, you know things are going well for you. How about when you feel angry, scared, or lonely? These feelings are signals to you that things are not going the way you would like.

"All people have times in their life when they do not like the feelings they are having. When that happens, it is still very important to allow yourself to feel those 'bad feelings' because they are a signal telling you that perhaps you should take some steps to change the situation. If you are unable to do anything to change the situation, perhaps you can talk about your 'bad feelings' to someone whom you care about and trust. It is very important always to remember that **all** feelings are O.K., even though we can't act on all of them. Emotions are one of the special things that make us human."

V. FEELINGS ACTIVITY AND DISCUSSION

A. For children approximately 4 to 8 years of age, use the prepared faces for this activity.

   1. Put faces on display, one at a time.
   2. As you display each face, ask the following questions of the group:
     a. What feeling does this face bring to mind?
     b. Have any of you ever felt this way? When?
     c. What does this feel like inside?
     d. How do you behave when you feel like this?
     e. What does it feel like to you when you see someone else looking like this face?

B. For children approximately 9 to 12 years of age, use the prepared cards for this activity.

   1. Spread cards out on a table, written side down.
   2. Ask each group member to draw a card at random.
   3. Ask each member to reveal to the group the feeling on the card, to tell the group if he or she has ever felt that way, and to talk about the circumstances or the situation that caused the feeling. Also ask:
     a. What does this feeling feel like inside?
     b. How do you behave when you feel like this?
     c. How does it make you feel when you think someone else feels like this?

C. Ask if group members have any questions or comments about feelings.

D. Then ask the following questions to help group members focus more specifically on feelings related to divorce:

   1. Ask the children what feelings they had when their parents got divorced.

2. Ask the children to draw a picture illustrating these feelings.
3. Ask the children to share their pictures with the group and to tell the group about their feelings.
4. As children share their pictures, ask the group members what they think each person can do about his or her feelings.

E. *Common Feelings Related to Divorce*

Every person has within him- or herself the ability to experience and express a range of human feelings. When children go through a divorce, they frequently experience several common feelings; two of the most powerful feelings are **sadness** and **anger**. Children accept and become comfortable with their feelings when they know that others are experiencing the same or similar emotions in reaction to similar situations. When children know that others share what they feel, it becomes acceptable to have those feelings. When children hear others express both good and bad feelings, they become comfortable in acknowledging and sharing their own feelings.

1. Ask the group members to tell you their feelings about their parents' divorce. Tell them you are going to make a list of all their feelings.
2. On a large piece of paper taped to the wall or on a chalkboard, write down the various feelings the children mention about divorce. Listen for some of the most common, including anger, hurt, loss, confusion, sadness, fear, worry, guilt, relief, shame, and embarrassment. If the children do not include all of the above feelings on their list, add them by asking, for example, "How about **confusion**, did any of you feel confused?"
3. Normalize the children's feelings by highlighting how common many of their feelings are. This will help the children accept their feelings as legitimate reactions to their situations, thus helping them feel better about themselves. Encourage the children to accept the fact that it is normal for people to have feelings, even strong feelings of anger.

Tell the children that their goal should be to recognize and express their feelings when they occur, rather than trying to deny a feeling and keep it all bottled up inside.

a. Read over the list of feelings on the newsprint or chalkboard. Ask the children to raise their hands if they have experienced the listed feeling. Put a mark near feelings for which **all** the children raise their hands.

b. Comment on the commonality of the feelings. For example: "I see that many of you share each of these feelings. I saw several hands go up for most feelings. You **all** seem to share the feelings X, Y, and Z" (read feelings you marked).

4. Reemphasize the main points of the mini-lecture: "You've all shared your feelings, which is very brave.

You've shared both good and bad feelings. These feelings are signals to what's going on in your lives right now. If you don't like a feeling you're having, that's O.K., because we all have feelings sometimes that we don't like. Perhaps you can talk to someone about that feeling. Also, in the weeks to come, we'll talk about some other ways to handle feelings you don't like. It's important to remember that all feelings are O.K.—they are those special things that make us human."

5. Optional exercise aimed at further normalizing feelings of divorce:

   a. For children 4 to 8 years of age, read *Dinosaurs Divorce* aloud.[1] Pages 6 through 10 are especially helpful in addressing feelings.

   b. For children 9 to 12 years of age, read *How Does It Feel When Your Parents Get Divorced?*[2] This book deals entirely with feelings associated with divorce. The text is brief and the book also includes helpful illustrations.

   c. Discuss the feelings expressed in these books in relation to feelings brought out by the group.

6. *Optional Exercise: Three Wishes*

   One way to assess the impact of the group on the children is to gather "before" and "after" examples of the thoughts, wishes, and feelings that preoccupy them. At this point, the children have taken part in two sessions and are often more tuned into personal and family issues. Tell the group members to imagine that a magical genie has appeared and has offered to grant them each three wishes. Ask the children to draw pictures illustrating the three wishes that they have.

   This exercise is repeated in Session 7 for comparison. It can be helpful to you later in determining if the children have made progress in addressing the psychological tasks of divorce. Progress is indicated if the wishes have become more realistic, constructive, self-oriented, and focused on future goals by the end of the group.

VI. SUMMARY OF SESSION

Review for the group the key ideas for this session:

A. Everyone has feelings

B. Some feelings we like to have and some we don't, but it's important to allow ourselves to "feel" all of our feelings because they are important signals.

C. It is important to recognize the feelings you have and to be able to "name" them. The most common feelings that children who experience divorce have are anger, hurt, relief, fear, sadness, confusion, loss, worry, and embarrassment. Be sure to include in the list common feelings that the children identified in the second part of the exercise described in Section V, E.

D. It is good to share feelings with people whom you care about and trust.

VII. ANTICIPATING THE NEXT SESSION

Tell the children that next week they will hear a story about a cat named Barney and that the group will talk about what happens to him. (If you use a different story in Session 3, indicate what you will be discussing.) Tell the children that they will also be doing an exercise about all the different things that have happened in their lives. Tell younger children to think about or ask parents when they were born, how many times they have moved, and what births or deaths have occurred in their families.

Note: Include the children's drawings in the children's divorce books. The group leader should also photocopy the list of common feelings assembled in part V, so that each child can have a copy for his or her book.

NOTES

1. Laurene Krasay Brown and Marc Brown, *Dinosaurs Divorce* (Boston: Little Brown and Company, 1986).

2. Terry Berger, *How Does It Feel When Your Parents Get Divorced?* (New York: Julian Messner, 1977).

Session 3
LOSSES

OBJECTIVES

- ✔ To help children see that loss is a universal experience both in nature and for all people
- ✔ To help children see that they and their families experience many losses in everyday living
- ✔ To help children identify the particular losses that most children experience in separation and divorce
- ✔ To normalize the feelings and reactions that are common in experiencing losses, such as sadness, anger, and guilt

MATERIALS

- ✔ Blank time lines or paper for the children to draw them on
- ✔ Black-covered box
- ✔ Crayons, pencils, or markers

BRIEF OUTLINE

   I. Mini-Lecture: Losses
  II. Group Discussion
 III. Time-Line Activity
  IV. "Black Box" Activity
   V. Summary of Session
  VI. Anticipating the Next Session

I.   MINI-LECTURE: LOSSES

"When we love someone, we get close to that person and enjoy the security that comes with knowing we are loved, too. We can get so close to people or pets or friends that we feel they truly become a part of us. We think about them, daydream about them, and look forward to all the good times we will share with them.

"Perhaps you've had a pet in your home that helped teach you how important it is to take care of someone you love. In many families, children are assigned special responsibilities, like feeding the cat or walking the dog or cleaning the hamster's cage. Perhaps some of you have had the sad experience of losing a pet when the pet died or got lost. Can you remember such a time? You probably felt very sad and helpless and even a little angry when you no longer had your pet. Maybe you had a feeling of emptiness when you first realized the pet was no longer there to cuddle or to play with you. It didn't seem to be the same, secure world as it was when the pet was alive.

"We all experience feelings of sadness and anger in losing someone or something important to us in many parts of our lives. Think for a moment about what happens in nature. All of nature is in a constant process of blooming and growing and dying and being reborn all over again. Every summer, fall, winter, and spring, nature goes through a cycle of growing and dying and growing again. We learn to count on this process. We have the same experience every day in seeing the dawn, the beginning of a new day; we see the day unfold with lots of activity. Toward the end of the afternoon the day slowly quiets down, and at dusk it becomes dark again and we fall asleep, waiting for a new day and new opportunities.

"In our group exercise today, we'll be talking about many of the common losses that children experience in separation and divorce. You have all had to let go of things that had meaning for you, like having two parents in your home. You may have had to move from your home or neighborhood, leaving behind friends, your school, pets, relatives who were close by, your own room, and activities you enjoyed. Possibly you may even have experienced changes due to a parent's loss of a job. You have all gone through many changes in your life and have had to adjust to new people, new places, and new routines. Anytime a family goes through changes, everyone in it can experience stress or difficulties. In our group today, we'll discuss how it feels to let go of things we love and how it feels to reach out and try to feel secure again with new people, places, and experiences in our lives."

II. GROUP DISCUSSION

When a child undergoes the separation and divorce of his or her parents, some of the immediate, personal losses may be too painful to discuss openly and directly. It is often easier for children to address issues of separation and loss through familiar stories. Classic children's literature and films often contain sympathetic characters who experience loss of a parent, feelings of loss and confusion, and a search to regain a secure living situation. Many children will find it less threatening at first to talk about a symbolic character than it is to discuss their personal feelings.

A. The group leader should read aloud *The Tenth Good Thing about Barney.*[1] In this book, a boy's pet cat, Barney, dies. The boy's mother challenges him to think of ten good things to remember about Barney. As the child fondly recalls what Barney meant to him, he realizes that the pleasant memories help ease the pain of losing his pet. He realizes that these memories will last longer than the pain and that he can carry the good memories into the future.

1. Discuss with group members their reactions to this book. (Although the book is designed for children aged 5 to 8 years, children in the 9-to-12 age group can relate to it also.) Ask questions such as the following:
   a. What feelings did the boy have about Barney's death?
   b. How could you tell he had these feelings? What did he do?
   c. How did people help him cope with his feelings?

      d. Who bothered him or made him angry?

      e. What meaning could the boy make out of Barney's death? What helped the boy remember Barney in a positive way?

      f. What did you like about the book? Why?

      g. What did you dislike about the book? Why?

  2. Ask the group members about experiences that they might have had with pets.

      a. What pets have you had?

      b. If you haven't had a pet, have you ever visited another family's home where you enjoyed their pet?

      c. How many of you remember losing a pet through death? Running away?

      d. What did it feel like when you lost a pet?

      e. Who or what helped you with your feelings?

B. If you feel more comfortable with storytelling, an alternative to using a children's book is to recount your own experiences with losing a pet or something valuable to you or to create your own imaginative story about a child losing a pet.

C. Many children today are familiar with classic fairy tales, movie plots, or Walt Disney characters. Another approach is to choose one of the following stories and ask the children to recount the story and discuss feelings having to do with losing someone or being separated from loved ones through the main characters of the story. Possibilities include:

1. Bambi
2. The Land Before Time
3. E.T.
4. Old Yeller
5. The Wizard of Oz
6. An American Tail
7. Star Wars
8. Home Alone

9. Sleeping Beauty
10. Peter Pan

III. TIME-LINE ACTIVITY

Many children feel as if they are alone in their experience of divorce and that no one else has experienced the losses they have endured. A time line is an excellent way to show children that each of them has had special experiences but that others have also undergone losses. A time line also implicitly demonstrates to them that people move on with their lives despite losses and family disruptions.

A. Ask the children to draw a horizontal line across a piece of paper midway between its top and bottom, leaving a small margin at either end. (To save time, you might prepare several blank time lines beforehand for the group to fill in.) Have them put a dot and the current calendar year at the far right side of the line. Then ask them to place a dot and the year of their birth at the far left side of the line. Over the dot, ask them to draw a star, signifying their birth. You might have to help younger children estimate their year of birth by subtracting their age from the current year. Finally, ask the children to place dots evenly across their time lines to indicate the intervening years.

B. Explain to the children that at this point, all the time lines look similar. But, as they add more dates and events, each line will become unique or "your own special time line."

C. Ask the children to mark their time lines as follows, to indicate significant events in their lives. Begin with occasions that are happy, or at least neutral, events for most children, then lead into more painful milestones. You might ask:

1. When did you start kindergarten? Place a capital letter "K" at that date.
2. If you went to nursery school, place an "N" by the year when you were three or four.

3.   Was a brother or sister born after you? Place a small star by that birth date.

4.   Has a pet joined your family since you were born? Place a "P" or the pet's name by the year it came to live with you.

5.   Did you ever take special vacations that you can remember? Place a "V" by those dates.

6.   Can you identify other happy events, such as winning a prize, being on a special team, or joining scouts? Make your own symbols or letter for these events.

7.   Can you remember any deaths of relatives or pets? Place an "X" by that date.

8.   Can you remember when your parents separated? Place an "S" on that date.

9.   Can you remember how many times you have moved since you were born? Put an "M" by the year of each move or, if you can't remember the date of every move, place the correct number of "M's" throughout your time line.

10.   When did your parents divorce? Place a "D" on the line by that date.

D.   Ask the children to look at their time lines and note all the changes that they have experienced. Then, to elicit from the children an understanding of the individual nature of their experiences, ask the group members to hold up their time lines and briefly describe them to the group. After each child has finished, comment on his or her time line. For instance, you might say, "I see you moved more than once in your life" or "You must be an older brother [sister]. How many babies were born after you?"

E.   When the children are finished, briefly summarize the ways in which their time lines are similar—most of the children will have experienced starting school and the acquisition of pets, for instance—and how they are different. For example, perhaps one child moved five times and two children only moved once.

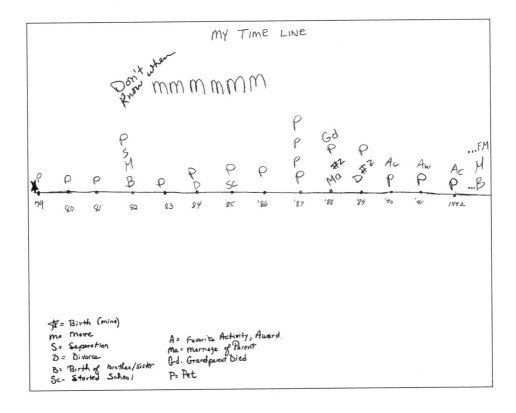

MY TIME LINE

Don't when Know

mm m mm M

P
S
M

P
P
P
Gd
P
P

P
P
P
Ma #2
P
D #2
Ac
P
Aw
P
...FM
Ac
P
M
...B

P   P   P   B   P   P
D   Sc   P   P

'79 80 81 82 83 84 '85 '86 '87 '88 '89 '90 '91 1992

✗ = Birth (mine)
m = Move
S = Separation
D = Divorce
B = Birth of brother/sister
Sc = Started School

A = Favorite Activity, Award.
Ma = Marriage of Parent
Gd = Grandparent Died
P = Pet

F. Now ask the children to look at their time lines and pick out all the changes that went with divorce—moves, giving up pets, and so forth. Encourage discussion about the emotional effects of these changes. For example, ask how a family move before a divorce is different from a move because of a divorce. Perhaps the child has had friends or cousins who moved because a parent got a job promotion and had to relocate. How was this different from moving due to divorce? How might the losses be similar?

For instance, if a move due to divorce results in the child living in a new city or different neighborhood, the child may be grappling with his or her greatest fear—the loss of one parent in daily life. Some other losses, however, such as losing friends or a familiar school, might be similar in both kinds of moves.

It is important for the leader to recognize that children of divorce may have had so many changes forced upon them that they feel overwhelmed. They may feel very little sense of control over the changes in their lives. Moreover, children may feel even more anger and sadness about losses due to divorce than about losses stemming from death or illness. This is because the child perceives that one or both parents had a **choice** in imposing changes (and consequent losses) on the child, whereas the child had no power to effect change.

Another way to stimulate discussion about the emotional correlates of losses due to divorce is to ask each group member to identify the event on his or her time line that caused the greatest anger, sadness, or hurt. The leader can balance the discussion by asking each child which event caused him or her to feel the greatest happiness or pride in achievement.

G. Remind the children that, despite their lives having many things in common, no one else in the world has a time line just like theirs. Their time lines will become part of their own special books about divorce. And their time lines show that they are all learning to cope and adapt to change, which makes them stronger.

IV. "BLACK BOX" ACTIVITY

It is important for the children to put an end to some of their feelings of sadness and anger stemming from losses due to divorce. They need to express their grief so they can eventually put it behind them and move on in their lives. Otherwise, children who hold onto their sadness and anger can become depressed or exhibit behavior problems. The "black box" exercise is designed to help the group members address their losses and acknowledge that these losses cannot be retrieved.

A. Tell the children, "You are going to have the opportunity to put a final end to those losses you have experienced in divorce. If you can say good-bye to those things that can never be regained, you will no longer feel so hurt by them. If you can free yourself of the hurt, you will be able to fill that space with new experiences."

B. Ask the children to think about losses associated with divorce that they have already identified and write on a piece of paper those that can never be regained—a home that was sold, a friend whom they moved away from, or the wish that their parents would get married again.

C. Tell the children that they are going to "let go" of these losses and bury them themselves. Ask each child to place his or her paper in the black box you brought to this session, or toss them away in the wastebasket. Explain to them that it is O.K. to feel sad about these losses or to cry if they want, because it is hard to say good-bye to things that you care about—just as it was hard for the boy in the story read at the beginning of the session to say good-bye to Barney.

D. Invite the children to hold the box or wastebasket together and carry it to a "hiding place" in the room, as if to bury it. Then tell them that after a funeral, people sometimes feel less sad through sharing their grief and supporting one another. They do this by talking about their losses and saying things such as "I'll be your friend," "I'm sorry you're feeling sad," or "Can I help you?" Invite the children to help one another cope with the loss by offering support and understanding.

The leader can conclude this exercise by asking the children to sit down and share with the group their thoughts and feelings about the funeral exercise.

V. SUMMARY OF SESSION

Review for the group the key ideas for this session:

A. If we love someone or something special, it hurts to lose that person or thing.

B. All people experience losses throughout their lives.

C. Children whose families are broken up by divorce have losses in common.

D. Children who experience losses also usually experience certain feelings in common, such as sadness, anger, guilt, and confusion.

E. If we can let go of some of the feelings attached to the losses we cannot regain, we will have new energy to reach out to new people and new experiences in our lives.

VI. ANTICIPATING THE NEXT SESSION

Tell the group that next week the group will write a creative story about a family experiencing separation and divorce. You will be using their ideas and artwork for the story.

NOTE

1. If you cannot find a copy of *The Tenth Good Thing about Barney* or wish to use another book, consult your local children's librarian for possible alternatives. Some additional book suggestions to use with children aged 5 to 10 are included in the resource list at the end of this session.

RESOURCE LIST

Children's books about experiencing loss in the family or in nature that can be used in connection with this session include:

1. Aliki Brandenberg, *The Two of Them*. New York: Greenwillow Books, 1979.

   A tender story about the special relationship between a young girl and her grandfather. The story begins when she is a baby and he cares for her. It concludes with the girl as an older child who cares for her now disabled and dying grandfather.

2. Margaret Wise Brown, *The Dead Bird*. New York: Young, Scott Books, 1958.

   The story recounts a group of young children's first experience with death when they discover a dead bird. They handle their sadness by having a funeral for the bird and tending its grave after its death.

3. Leo Buscaglia, *The Fall of Freddie the Leaf*. New York: Holt, Rinehart and Winston, 1982.

   This book helps children tie the concept of death to the life cycle of nature. Freddie the Leaf falls from his tree and finds himself completing the life cycle.

4. Tomie dePaola, *Nana Upstairs and Nana Downstairs*. New York: G. P. Putnam's Sons, 1973.

   Tommy, a young boy, is part of a multigenerational family. First, he experiences the death of a great grandmother when he is young. As a man, he experiences the death of his grandmother and thinks about the special relationship he had with both.

5. Joan Fassler, *My Grandpa Died Today*. New York: Human Services Press, 1971.

    The story is a realistic account of the events around the death of a boy's grandfather. By the end of the story, the child accepts the absence of this special grandparent.

6. Miska Miles, *Annie and the Old One*. New York: Little, Brown and Co., 1971.

    This is a sweet story about a young Navajo girl who realizes that her grandmother is dying. The child tries to put off the inevitable death, but her grandmother helps her accept the loss as part of nature's life cycle.

7. Sarah Stein, *About Dying*. New York: Walker and Company, 1974.

    Two young children, Eric and Jane, first experience the death of a pet bird, later followed by the death of their grandfather. The story and pictures, aimed at the young reader, are simple and vivid. A companion text for parents or other adults parallels the story and provides insight into how to discuss losses with children.

8. Susan Varley, *Badger's Parting Gifts*. New York: Lothrop, Lee and Shepard Books, 1984.

    In a moving tale of friendship, a kindly old badger dies and his friends share their sadness and grief by remembering everything he taught them. The memories of the badger's gifts bring consolation and acceptance to his friends.

Session 4

ACCEPTANCE OF DIVORCE

OBJECTIVES

✔ To introduce the effects that divorce has on a family
✔ To educate the children about the high incidence of divorce in the population so that they feel less stigmatized
✔ To help the children identify common feelings and experiences of families undergoing divorce
✔ To lessen the children's feelings of isolation through group identification and discussion of common reactions

MATERIALS

✔ *Dinosaurs Divorce*
✔ Drawing paper and crayons, pencils, or colored markers

BRIEF OUTLINE

I. Opening the Session
II. Fictional Divorce Story
III. Creation of Family Divorce Story
IV. Drawing Exercise
V. Summary of Session
VI. Anticipating the Next Session

I. OPENING THE SESSION

A. Briefly summarize the previous session. Ask if the children have any questions or comments concerning the last session.

B. Present a brief outline of material to be covered in this session. "Today we will be having fun by writing our own creative story about divorce. To help us with ideas for the story, we'll hear a story that another author has written. Each of you will have a chance to contribute to *our* story. Then we'll draw pictures to accompany our story. The group story and your pictures will be placed in your personal book about divorce."

II. FICTIONAL DIVORCE STORY

A. Explain the group story activity:
"Today we have a creative activity to give each of you a chance to contribute to a special story about a family facing divorce. Your story will be different from any other story in the world. Some groups have even asked their schools or churches to publish their stories.

"Most cartoons, fables, and fairy tales tell their stories through animal figures. A popular book that does this is *Dinosaurs Divorce*, which I'm going to read from today. Then, picking a particular animal family, we can have fun by creating a story about them and having anything we want to happen happen to this family. Let's give it a try and you'll see how creative you can be.

"As I read this story, think about which characters you like or dislike. Is this family's experience anything like your own? Or is it very different? Ideas from this story can help you think about ideas for the group story."

B. Read the story *Dinosaurs Divorce* to the group. If you are pressed for time, the first chapter alone lends itself well to group discussion. If you prefer, you can substitute a story composed by a previous children's group. Two examples are included at the end of this chapter. Or you can compose your own creative story before the session, incorporating information such as names, ages, and occupations of family members; problems that arose between the parents and what happened to the family as a result of those problems; how the children felt and reacted to these circumstances; and what happened to the children when the parents split up. You might mention the post-divorce outcome, for example, one parent married a new partner who already had children, whereas the other parent never dated and remained bitter about the divorce.

C. *Discussion*

Elicit reactions to the story from the children. Based on your evaluation of the group's readiness, questions can be disguised by referring impersonally to the animals in the story, or questions can be more personal and direct—"Which character did you like the best?" versus "Which character was most like yourself?" Questions can include:

1. Which character was most like yourself? Least like yourself? Why?
2. Did your family experience anything that happened to the animal family? How was your experience different?
3. What feelings did the children in this family experience?
4. In your own words, tell why this family had a divorce.

III. CREATION OF FAMILY DIVORCE STORY

A. Challenge the group to write their own special story about a family experiencing separation and divorce. You can utilize a blackboard, flipchart, or newsprint paper to write down ideas as the children offer them. The following questions can help you to get the children started:

1. What kind of animal family is this? What are **their** favorite animals?

2. What is their last name? (Try to match the name with the animal group—i.e., Mr. and Mrs. Scratchy for a cat family.)

3. What are the names and ages of the parents? The children? How many members should this family have?

4. What does the father do for a living? The mother? (For fun, try to match a job with the animal the children choose, for example, thoroughbred racehorse for a horse family or an underwater plumber for a fish family.)

5. Where does the family live? Encourage the children to be imaginative—say, the North Pole or Hawaii or a cave hidden in a mountain.

6. Where do the children go to school?

7. What starts happening in this family that tells you there may be a separation or divorce coming? Do the parents argue? Does one parent leave? Do the children get into trouble at school?

8. What brings about the actual separation? Does one parent leave?

9. What happens to the children when the parents separate? Where do they live?

10. When does the family go from separation to divorce? When is the divorce final?

11. What happens to each family member when they first experience divorce?

12. What happens to each family member five years later?

13. What is the end of the story? How would you like to see this family in five years?

Note: This question often opens up discussion of an important issue. Many children fantasize that their parents will get back together again. You can use this opportunity to tell your group that most children hope that their parents will reunite, even though it is very unlikely that this will occur. You might ask them to supply two story endings, one a fantasy or wishful ending and the other a realistic conclusion acknowledging change and new life patterns after the marital break-up. If you elicit two endings, ask the group which ending they feel is more comfortable to them. A child's choice of a fantasy or reality ending can indicate how the child is coping with divorce.

B. Finalize the story by seeking a consensus answer to each question asked. Give all of the children an opportunity to contribute ideas for the story and participate in the final decision by using a group vote to select one response to each question. This process usually generates fun, enthusiasm, and support as members agree on ideas for each segment. By voting on an idea, even quiet children are drawn into the group process. By the end of the story, each member should feel partially responsible for the story that was created. Based on the voting, the leader should compose the story in written form to be passed out at the next meeting as a reward to the children for their creative efforts.

C. *Discussion of Group Story*
    Now, if you still have time, ask the children about their reactions to the story they have just created. Questions might include:

    1. Did you identify with any child in our story? Which one? Why?
    2. Did either of your parents seem like the parents in our story? How?
    3. Did your family experience any events like those in our story?
    4. Do you know any families like the family in our story? Could you tell us about their experience?
    5. What is the funniest part of the story? Why?
    6. What is the saddest part of the story? Why?
    7. What would help the children in our story to cope with separation and divorce?

    Note: Group leaders may want to allow extra time for discussing the last question, as the children may have written a story filled with difficult problems and issues. In the context of discussing coping strategies, this would be a good time to remind the group of the overall themes of the workshop:

a. All families are important. Children should try to have contact with both parents, if possible, after the divorce. Also, continued contact with other family members and relatives can help provide support for the child and ease his or her pain stemming from losses.

b. The children can find trusted people to talk to about their problems, such as teachers, relatives, clergy, counselors, and friends.

c. Activities that children enjoy, like sports or scouting, can help them cope with stress.

d. If parents do things that worry or bother them, the children should try to find ways to tell their parents about this.

IV. DRAWING EXERCISE

A. Pass out paper and crayons to the children. Ask them to draw a picture about the story that the group has just created.

B. Ask the children to share their pictures with the group and briefly describe their feelings about and reactions to the story. Ask what affected them the most.

V. SUMMARY OF SESSION

Review for the group the key ideas for this session.

A. Every family experiencing separation and divorce goes through a series of changes, just like the animal families did in our divorce story today.

B. Part of accepting divorce within a family is learning to live with the consequences of change and the new life-style that divorce brings to each family member.

C. Talking with others about troubling experiences often helps people understand themselves better and feel better about difficult situations such as divorce. Each of you can gain comfort in accepting the changes in your life when you share your own story with children who face similar transitions.

D. Like the animal family in our story, we look forward to a future in which we can help bring about the changes we want for our selves and our families.

VI. ANTICIPATING THE NEXT SESSION

"During the next week, think about the challenges you faced in dealing with the many changes that divorce brought into your life. We'll talk about the wish many children have that their parents will somehow get back together again, even when the children know this will probably never happen. We'll also tackle another important question that children often ask: 'Was I to blame for my parents' divorce?'"

SAMPLE STORIES

The Cat Family Story

Once there was a cat family, headed by Mr. and Mrs. Scratchy. Mr. Scratchy was 28 and Mrs. Scratchy was 25. They had five kittens whose names were Star, Silly, Skunky, Claws, and Puffy. They lived in a barn on a farm in Africa. Mr. Scratchy was a fisherman. Mrs. Scratchy was a mouse-catcher. The kittens played with yarn balls, messed up the house, broke windows, and played seesaw. Once they had an ice cream food fight. The kittens had such a big fight that they ran away.

The parents were unhappy. They fought over the kittens and who would get them if they split up. The parents didn't like each other any more and sometimes they hit one another. Sometimes they threw fish and mice at each other.

The Scratchy family finally got a separation. Mrs. Scratchy took Puffy, Skunky, and Star and moved to Tatamy, Pennsylvania. Mr. Scratchy took Claws and Silly and moved to Atlantic City, New Jersey. Mr. Scratchy soon hit the jackpot at a casino. Then both parents won the lottery. The kittens cried and cried when their parents wouldn't get back together again. They eventually had a big divorce and the kittens cried for seven years. Some of the kittens switched homes.

A Fish Family Story

Once there was a fish family named the Guppies. Mr. Guppie was 34; Mrs. Guppie was 33. Ritchie Guppie was 10 and Carrie Guppie was 4. The Guppies lived under a rock in the ocean in Florida. Mr. Guppie was a plumber. He was also on the city council, so he was very busy. Mrs. Guppie was a housewife who babysat for 12 baby fish after school, including Ritchie and Carrie. Ritchie was in the fourth grade at Slimey Fish Elementary School. Carrie stayed home and bugged Mom.

Then problems came. Dad was never home and then he lost his job. Mom wanted to get a job as a teacher, but Dad said, "No!" Mr. and Mrs. Guppie started arguing. Mr. Guppie wanted Mrs. Guppie home with the children. They fought over money. Dad started drinking and Mom took sleeping pills. Ritchie started getting into trouble at school for things like throwing food in the lunchroom. He got a detention. Carrie became a brat, throwing toys and pulling the fins of the other fish.

So the parents separated. Ritchie went to live with Mr. Guppie and Carrie stayed with Mrs. Guppie. Sometimes Ritchie and Carrie went to live with relatives. But they got into trouble at the relatives' homes when they began swearing and playing pranks on the telephone. Mom finally got a full-time job teaching, so Carrie went to a day-care center. Before long, Mom got into trouble on her new job because the sleeping pills made her drowsy during the day.

Finally Mr. and Mrs. Guppie got a divorce. Mrs. Guppie then had a new boyfriend. They got married and had two baby fish of their own. Mr. Guppie continued to work hard and he became the president of the undersea world. Eventually they all lived happily ever after.

Session 5
DEALING WITH DIVORCE

OBJECTIVES

✔ To help children relinquish feelings of self-blame
✔ To help children gain understanding about what constitutes a good relationship and what may have contributed to the dissolution of their parents' marriage
✔ To help members assess the common fantasy that their parents will reunite

MATERIALS

✔ Crayons, pencils, or markers
✔ Copies of sentence completion exercise or sentence completion exercise written on chalkboard or newsprint
✔ Candles and matches

BRIEF OUTLINE

I. Mini-Lecture: Self-Blame
II. What's a Marriage?
III. Permanence and Self-Blame: Sentence Completion Exercise
IV. Candle Ritual
V. Summary of Session
VI. Anticipating the Next Session

I.   MINI-LECTURE: SELF-BLAME

"The first reaction of many children when they hear that their parents are thinking about divorce is, 'It's my fault.' This is a very common feeling. Some children say this out loud and share their feeling with others. Some children don't say it, but they still think and feel that they are to blame. They recall all of the things that they may have done in the past that upset their parents and they wish none of that had happened. Many children feel that their parents are divorcing because Mom or Dad got mad when they misbehaved, didn't keep their room clean, or didn't get good enough grades at school. Children may think, 'If I had been more lovable, Mom or Dad would have stayed home more and we could have been a happy family.' Children start to think of the times that they heard their parents fighting and they feel bad that they couldn't help out or stop the fights. There are many ways that children blame themselves for their parents' divorce, and these thoughts make children feel sad, unloved, and guilty.

"Parents do **not** divorce because of their children or the things that children do. All children misbehave at one time or another, get into trouble, or don't clean up after themselves as they are told. These things do **not** cause parents to divorce. Children can't stop parents from fighting, nor should they have to. Children can't always fix things that are wrong in a family. Children can't always 'make things better' when they see a parent crying, hurt, or upset.

"Parents get divorced because they no longer have the same feelings for each other that they had when they decided to get married. Sometimes things happen to change the way people feel about each other. When feelings change, sometimes people can't get along with each other as peacefully as they could before. They find it hard to cooperate in order to work things out or solve problems.

"Did you ever have a best friend? By this I mean someone you liked a whole lot; someone you had fun with; someone you trusted; someone who you thought would be your best friend forever. Then maybe something happened after a while that changed your feelings about this person. Maybe he lied to you or told someone else a secret you shared. Maybe she got bossy after a while and wouldn't let you make any decisions. Maybe he decided that he liked to play with someone else more than with you. What a surprise! You thought you'd be best friends forever. These kinds of things happen to grownups, too. They don't plan it, but sometimes parents behave in ways that change the way they feel about each other. When this happens, it gets harder and harder for them to work together for the good of the family. The parents may fight more or talk less to each other, and their feelings about each other get more and more damaged. This is why parents may decide to get divorced—all because of things that happen between the **two** of them. Adult troubles, not children, may lead parents to decide to separate. When parents can't find ways to solve the problems between them, they may get a divorce."

II. WHAT'S A MARRIAGE?

A. Older children, nine years of age and older, usually have some ideas about the nature of relationships. Pre-teens will have a lot of comments to contribute to the following exercises. If your group is mostly composed of children who are younger than nine years, skip the exercise described in the following section and follow the alternative one given in section D.

B. Ask the group for ideas in response to the question "What makes a marriage work?" Write their suggestions on a chalkboard or on newsprint. As ideas are presented, lead the group in discussion of why each suggestion is necessary or important in a marriage. Group members may mention first the intangibles of relationships—love, commitment, loyalty, cooperation, teamwork, and respect. Try to elicit from them the tangible ingredients as well, such as money to pay bills, a place to live, and so forth. Encourage the children to consider what is essential to a good relationship in order to expand their understanding of how a marriage works or fails. Among the comments from a group of 10- to 12-year-olds were planning, respect, being positive, liking or loving the other person, making each other feel good.

C. Now ask the children to discuss the question "What causes divorce?" Responses to this question from the aforementioned group of 10- to 12-year-olds were money took over, my parents got bored, one fell in love with another person, different educations, they never loved each other, and my parent drank a lot. It is important to emphasize in the group discussion of this question that the children's parents had their own problems and that the children are not to blame for their parents' divorce.

D. Children younger than nine years of age may know less about relationships and will find the previous exercise difficult. But most of them will have attended a wedding at some point in their lives or will have seen a wedding portrayed on television or in a movie. If your group is composed of younger children, ask the group instead what a marriage ceremony is like and what is said at the ceremony. The point is to get the children to think of why and how their parents got married.

It is important for the children to realize that there was a time when their parents loved each other and had a happy relationship. Given all the problems divorce brings to a family, children need to remember that their parents' marriage was not always troubled. This exercise helps children to salvage some of the positive qualities that existed in their parents' relationship and family life. You may have to fill in the blanks about what goes on at a wedding ceremony. Depending on how knowledgeable your group is about marriage ceremonies, you may have to teach them about marriage vows and how people feel about each other when they get married as the group proceeds to answer these questions. This discussion will help you decide whether they are familiar enough with wedding ceremonies to complete the exercise by (1) role playing or enacting their parents' marriage ceremony or (2) drawing a picture of their parents' wedding.

E. Next, ask the children to tell you why people get divorced. Remember, as group members chime in with their comments, that the issue you are addressing is the children's natural instinct to blame themselves. Gently correct any comments that suggest a child is to blame and reinforce the points that you presented in the mini-lecture at the beginning of this session.

Children may tell you that parents in general get divorced because they don't love each other anymore or they fight all the time. Probably you will also hear specific personal comments about a child's parents, such as "My father lost his job again and again," "My mother fell in love with someone else," "My father hit my mother." Let the children know that these things happen in many families. Emphasize that these are problems that parents have that may lead to divorce and that ***adult problems, not children, cause divorce.***

F. If you feel the children are capable of applying their ideas about divorce to a role play, ask them to make up a "divorce ceremony." What might people say to each other if they had a divorce ceremony? Where would it be held? Who would come? A role play of a divorce ceremony may not only clarify for the child reasons that people divorce, but may also address the second major issue tackled in this session, namely, the ***permanence*** of divorce. Symbolically enacting a parental divorce ceremony may help the children accept the fact that divorce is permanent. If your group does not seem capable of this role play because of their maturity or knowledge level, encourage them to imagine what a divorce ceremony might be like and ask them to draw a picture of an imaginary divorce ceremony with their parents in it.

III. PERMANENCE AND SELF-BLAME

The issues of the permanence of divorce and alleviating the feelings of self-blame are so central to divorce adjustment and recovery for a child that it is important to tackle these issues more than once in a variety of ways.

In addition to the exercises suggested so far, we have found the following sentence-completion test to be helpful. Sometimes the children have never been asked these questions directly, yet their responses may be very helpful to them in coping with divorce. Leaders can ask the group members to fill out individual sentence-completion tests on photocopied sheets of paper or pose the questions to the group by writing them on a chalkboard or newsprint.

SENTENCE COMPLETION

1. I first realized that my parents were having troubles with each other when _____
    _____

2. As troubles developed between my parents, I saw some things happen in my family like _____
    _____

3. I heard them say things like _____

4. When my parents first told me about the divorce, I felt _____
    _____

5. When I had to tell my friends that my parents were separating, I felt
    _____

6. The biggest changes that I faced when my parents separated or divorced were _____
    _____

7. When one parent moved out, I worried that _____
    _____

8. What helped me get by and cope when my parents separated was
    _____
    _____

9.   The person who understood me best through that time was _____

10.   I still hope my parents might get back together when I _____
_____

11.   I realize that my parents will not get back together when I _____
_____

12.   What helps me accept my new life with parents in separate homes is
_____
_____

This exercise will generate a lot of information and emotions. The questions require group members to face the difficult realities of separation and divorce but also challenge them to find ways to cope with the changes that have occurred. Group leaders may discuss all of the items or select a few to talk about, depending on the time available and the willingness of the children to share their experiences. It is rewarding for the children to hear the answers offered by their peers, as it lessens their own burdens and gives them hope that they can handle the situation and cope with the outcome. If the children are initially reluctant to share their answers, leaders can stimulate discussion by offering examples of answers given in other groups or from the leaders' own experience with other children.

IV. CANDLE RITUAL

A.   Clinging to the fantasy that divorced parents will eventually reunite often distances a child from the reality of the world he or she inhabits. It may make the child emotionally unavailable in other relationships that have positive things to offer, such as the affection of a new stepfather or stepmother, the social stimulus of stepsiblings, or the positive interaction with teachers and community leaders who can serve as role models. Also, many children firmly believe that they can love only one parent once their parents separate. In other words, the children feel they must choose whom they will love and whose relationship they must sacrifice. Often, parents' actions encourage the child to feel he or she must prefer one parent over the other. A troubled noncustodial parent might convince a young child that he or she must not develop positive feelings for a new stepparent or stepsiblings. It is important for the group leader to communicate to the children that even though their parents are apart, it is O.K. still to love both of them. The group leader should point out that each of us has the potential to love many people in the course of life and that loving a stepparent will not lessen the loving feelings for parents.

B. A moving and powerful exercise to communicate these ideas to children is Claudia Jewett's candle ritual,[1] which we have adapted for use with children of divorce groups. This exercise illustrates for the children that love can not only survive separation and divorce, it might even grow and multiply with new relationships that come into the children's lives. The leader must familiarize him- or herself with the family constellation of each child involved in order to escort the child through the exercise. The candle ritual reaffirms the child's lovability and his or her ability to love others. It gives the child the freedom and permission to love both parents, and to extend that love to others who enter his or her life. The following is a general example of the ritual, which should be tailored to the child's personal situation when enacted.

C. As you light the first candle, tell the child that this represents him or her. Say, "You were born with the ability to receive love and to give love to others. This ability is a special gift that you have, a gift that glows and makes you feel wonderful." Appreciate the candle's warm glow as you continue: "When you were very little, a tiny baby, your mom probably took care of you most of the time. She fed you and held you and made you feel more wonderful. This candle is your mother." Light a second candle representing the child's mother. "See how your love for each other makes more love light and things glow and feel warmer? Then your dad helped to take care of you, too. He held you and helped feed and bathe you. He smiled at you and showed you love. Together, you lit another love light." Light a third candle that represents the child's father.

Then, depending on events in the child's life, you might say, "Mother and Father started having problems between them and their feelings about each other changed. Your dad moved out of the house and got his own place to live." Move the candle representing the father a distance away. "Even though he lives somewhere else, his love light still glows for you and yours still glows for him. Even though you are apart, see how your light continues to glow and see how his love light continues to glow for you."

If the situation warrants, you may want to refer to new relationships in the child's life. "Now Mom is marrying John. Even though he can never replace your father, John is another person in your life whom you can care about and who can care about you." Light another candle representing the stepfather. "You can see that the more caring there is, the more light and warmth there is around you. You can see that caring for John need not affect loving your father. When you visit your father, your love lights burn together as they always did, and they continue to glow for each other when you are apart." Move the appropriate candles back and forth to indicate these changes.

Continue along these lines to fit each child's new family constellation. The ritual helps free the children symbolically to love and care for new people in their lives while securing the feelings of love that they have for their parents. Because this exercise is a metaphor for feelings of love, it is important at the end to tell the children that the candles and their lights were used to represent love and caring. Especially with young children, remind them that the real love exists apart from the candle and that blowing out the candle at the conclusion of the exercise will never make real love go away. Ask the children if they understand this as you refer to each of the representative candles. Assess their understanding by asking if they are ready to help you blow out the candle because the exercise is complete for the day.

V. SUMMARY OF SESSION

Review for the group the key ideas covered in this session:

A. Adult problems lead to divorce. Children do ***not*** cause their parents' divorce.

B. Divorce is permanent. Wishing your parents will get back together will ***not*** make it happen and often causes you to miss out on other good relationships that come along.

C. Even though your parents are apart, you have the right to love both of them, even if they have stopped loving each other.

VI. ANTICIPATING THE NEXT SESSION

Tell the group that next week they will participate in exercises and play games aimed at identifying what bothers them most about their families getting divorced and what they can do to help themselves.

NOTE

1. Claudia Jewett, *Helping Children Cope with Separation and Loss* (Harvard, MA: Harvard Common Press, 1982), pp. 17–18.

Session 6

LIVING WITH DIVORCE

OBJECTIVES

✔ Help children identify the concerns and problems that most children face when their parents divorce
✔ Provide an opportunity for the children anonymously to acknowledge the problems they have experienced in their own families
✔ Help children express the characteristic feelings and reactions that arise from facing their problems related to the divorce
✔ Build group cohesion and sense of mutual understanding as children assist one another in drawing or acting out their special concerns
✔ Help the children to cope better with common problems by sharing solutions

MATERIALS

✔ "Concerns of Children of Divorce" Questionnaire
✔ Newsprint, drawing paper, and crayons or colored markers

BRIEF OUTLINE

   I. Mini-Lecture: Living with Divorce
  II. Activity: Concerns of Children of Divorce
 III. Summary of Session
 IV. Anticipating the Next Session

I.   MINI-LECTURE: LIVING WITH DIVORCE

"In our last session, we talked about the various ways that children deal with divorce in their families and learn to accept the many changes they experience. Today we'll look at how you must learn to live with these changes.

"A popular book written by a well-known child psychiatrist, Dr. Richard Gardner, has helped many children cope with divorce. This book is called *The Boys and Girls Book about Divorce*.[1] Most children say that after they read his book they feel much better because he writes about concerns they have but don't know how to talk about with their parents.

"Remember the creative story that we wrote two weeks ago? Think again about all the changes children have to learn to live with in connection with divorce:

A.   "Most children begin to recognize that one or both of their parents are unhappy with their marriage.

B.   "Usually one parent leaves the home and lives in a new home. The child must now 'visit' with the parent who left.

C.   "When parents separate or divorce, they often have money problems. This may lead to one parent moving to another home or both parents having to work more.

D.   "You have to learn to manage strong feelings and reactions, like anger, sadness, or frustration.

E.   "You may have different rules and routines to follow in the separate homes of your parents.

F.   "You may have a new stepparent and stepbrothers or stepsisters in your future.

G. "Your parents have to learn to share you, especially on holidays, birthdays, and vacations.

"Today you will answer a questionnaire designed on the basis of concerns expressed in Dr. Gardner's book. You may be surprised at how many of you will check off the same concerns. I hope that it will help you see that you are not alone in facing the many adjustments you must make in order to live with the consequences of divorce in your family.

"Part of living with divorce is realizing that helpful solutions exist for many of the concerns and problems you face. Many children initially feel overwhelmed or helpless when their family starts changing. But they find ways to feel secure again and to help themselves and their families move in a positive direction.

"Even though it may be hard at first, you can learn to understand your problems and feelings and share them with adults you trust. You may want to join activities or pursue hobbies you enjoy and find new routines that help you stay happy in the separate homes of your parents. Today, we'll help one another think of positive ways to solve the problems that come with living with divorce."

II. ACTIVITY: CONCERNS OF CHILDREN OF DIVORCE

A. Distribute the questionnaire "Concerns of Children of Divorce."

1. Ask the children to read each sentence and put a check mark by the statements that are true for them. (Some groups may feel more comfortable writing "yes" or "no" in the blank space in front of the statement.) With younger children, read each question aloud and check to see that they are able to follow each item and mark it appropriately.

2. Children may or may not want to sign their names to this questionnaire. Some of the questions are personal, and the children may want their answers to be confidential and anonymous.

B. Ask the children to turn their questionnaires in to you.

1. Tally their responses on a blank questionnaire. Before you
    tally the responses, provide group members with a piece of
    paper and pencils or crayons. Ask them to draw a picture or a
    symbol of one of their concerns regarding living with divorce.
    Explain that the group will soon be role playing or playing a
    game called "Win-Lose-Draw" from the concerns they all list-
    ed. This gives them a chance to practice what they might draw
    or act out for the group in subsequent exercises. For example, a
    child who misses his or her father might draw a picture of a cry-
    ing child waving to a father who is driving away.
2. Share with the group the "top vote-getters," so the children can
    see how their responses compare with those of other members.
3. Write the top vote-getters on a chalkboard or piece of
    newsprint so the group members can review them. Or return
    the questionnaires to the group members and ask them to
    mark the group tally next to their own responses. Collect the
    questionnaires when the children are done so the checklists
    can be included in the participants' books. Ask the children
    if they are comfortable including the questionnaires in their
    books where their parents can read them. If the children
    wish to keep their responses private, one option for the lead-
    er is to place a blank questionnaire in each of the books so
    that parents can ask their children the questions themselves.

C. Role-Play of the Common Concerns

1. Ask for volunteers who would like to act out a common
    concern from the questionnaire results to see if the group
    members can guess it as in the game "Charades."
2. The presenter may choose any item on the list of top vote-
    getters, choose another response from his or her own list, or
    role play a concern that wasn't covered on the question-
    naire, such as, "I have a hard time with my stepbrothers or
    stepsisters."

3. The presenter can choose other group members, including the leader, to help him or her enact the role play.

4. Have the "actors" present their scene. As their skit progresses, keep asking the children if they can guess what the concern is. Ask questions like "How does his face look?" or "Whom is this person dealing with?"

5. Once the scene is over and its subject uncovered, ask the presenters to role play the same problem with a helpful solution. Before they begin, you may want to elicit ideas from the other group members about what the solution might be.

6. After this role play is finished, highlight the solution to the problem and ask the group members to remember it. You may want to make a list of the other possible solutions mentioned earlier, noting that no one "right" answer exists to problems like the one presented to the group, and alternative solutions should always be considered.

D. Play "Win-Lose-Draw"

1. Ask each child to select a concern from the list or one not included on the list.
2. Have the children take turns going to a chalkboard or a piece of newsprint and draw a picture or symbol of that concern.
3. Help the group guess the meaning of each picture. Ask questions like "Does the person have a smile or a frown?" "Is it an adult or a child?" "Is it male or female?" Encourage the children to make guesses as each "artist" draws the picture.
4. After the group members guess the problem, ask them if others among them share the same problem.
5. Elicit ideas about what a solution to the problem might be. Ask the artist to try to draw a solution or have the artist pick a volunteer to help him or her resolve the problem.
6. After the drawing exercise is completed, highlight the solution to the problem and ask the group members to remember it. You may want to make a list of other solutions that were suggested by the group members.

III. SUMMARY OF SESSION

Review for the group the key ideas elicited during this session.

A. You aren't alone in the problems you face as your family goes through the changes associated with separation and divorce.

B. Each problem that you face has a solution waiting to be discovered.

C. It often helps to look at how other children work out solutions to their problems.

D. If you find solutions that help you, pass them along to another child who is in the midst of a similar difficulty.

E. Remember, almost half of all American children will experience divorce in the family at one time or another. So many of your friends and classmates may also be trying to find new ways to live in a family experiencing divorce. They can be a source of help to you, and you can be of help to them.

IV. ANTICIPATING THE NEXT SESSION

"In our next session, we'll talk about how important it is to find someone you trust to talk with about your concerns and problems having to do with divorce. We'll also draw an 'activity pie,' so think about all the activities you enjoy that take your mind off other concerns."

NOTE

1. Richard Gardner, *The Boys and Girls Book about Divorce* (New York: Bantam, 1971).

CONCERNS OF CHILDREN OF DIVORCE

_____ 1. Sometimes I try to hide my sadness.

_____ 2. Sometimes I try to hide my anger at my mother.

_____ 3. Sometimes I try to hide my anger at my father.

_____ 4. I miss my father.

_____ 5. I miss my mother.

_____ 6. I wish my parents would get back together.

_____ 7. Sometimes I think my parents divorced because of me.

_____ 8. Sometimes I do bad things to get attention.

_____ 9. Sometimes I'm afraid I'll be left alone.

_____10. I wish my mother or father would get married again.

_____11. I wish my mom wouldn't say bad things about my father.

_____12. I wish my father wouldn't say bad things about my mother.

_____13. It bothers me when my mother (father) goes on a date.

_____14. I wish I could change the visitation schedule.

_____15. Sometimes I play my mother against my father.

_____16. Sometimes I play my father against my mother.

_____17. At times my parents use me as a weapon.

_____18. Sometimes I'm used as a spy or tattletale.

_____19. Sometimes it's difficult to get along with my stepfather.

_____20. Sometimes it's difficult to get along with my stepmother.

_____21. I worry about money in our family.

_____22. Sometimes I'm ashamed that my parents are divorced.

_____23. I wish I could see my mother (father) more.

Session 7

POSITIVE COPING MECHANISMS

OBJECTIVES

✔ Help the children learn ways to cope with negative feelings
✔ Teach children that involvement in activities helps to create balance in their lives
✔ Teach children that communicating with people they trust helps to create security in their lives

MATERIALS

✔ A circular object such as a paper plate colored red for the children to focus on during the first exercise
✔ Paper and colored crayons or markers

BRIEF OUTLINE

  I. Focus Exercise
 II. Mini-Lecture: Taking Your Mind Off It
III. Activity-Pie Exercise
 IV. Mini-Lecture: Talking It Over
  V. Trust-Circles Exercise
 VI. Mini-Lecture: Family Meetings
VII. Optional Exercise: Three Wishes (repeat)
VIII. Summary of Session
 IX. Anticipating the Next Session

I. FOCUS EXERCISE

A. Hold up the red circle that you have brought with you to the group and ask the children to focus on it. Tell them you want them to continue to think about the circle throughout the following exercise. Hold it up for approximately 30 seconds. Then put the circle away.

B. Tell the children to stand up and explain to them that you are going to play a game similar to "Simon Says." Stress that the children need only to listen and follow you; the game has no tricks and no winners or losers.

C. Begin to touch various parts of your body, jump on one foot, do jumping jacks, and so forth, encouraging the children to follow along. Do the exercise rapidly for about five minutes.

D. When you stop, ask the children if any of them remembered to think about the red circle during the exercise. Most of the children will probably say no, which will allow you to make the transition to the mini-lecture on overcoming negative or bad feelings that follows.

II. MINI-LECTURE: TAKING YOUR MIND OFF IT

"It's very difficult for us to think about two different things at the same time. Even though I asked you to continue thinking about the red circle during the exercise, most of you were unable to do so because you were busy thinking about and following my instructions. Being involved in activities takes our mind off other things and helps us cope with things in our lives that cause negative or bad feelings. If you're feeling sad because you didn't get to visit your dad over the weekend, playing ball with your friends won't make the sadness go away. But having fun will help you to stop thinking about your disappointment for a while, and it will replace the sad feelings with some happy feelings."

III. ACTIVITY-PIE EXERCISE

A. Pass out paper and markers.

B. Ask the children to draw a big circle, or pie, on the paper and then divide the pie into slices. Each slice will represent an activity that they enjoy, so ask the group members to draw a picture in each slice that depicts a favorite activity.

C. Ask the children to share their activity pies with the group, high-lighting the activities that they enjoy the most.

D. As the children talk about their activities, make a list of activities mentioned on the chalkboard or flip chart to illustrate the range of activities that group members engage in.

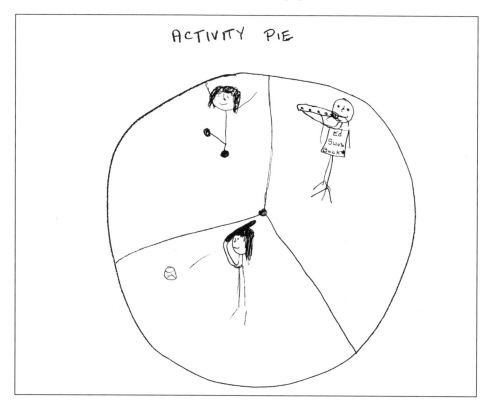

E.   After the children are finished, use the list to stress the variety of activities in which they take part. You may wish to suggest that some of them may want to try a new activity based on what they heard from the group.

IV.   MINI-LECTURE: TALKING IT OVER

"Another very good way to cope with negative feelings is to talk about your feelings with someone you trust. Talking helps to get feelings out into the open, and sometimes just doing that makes you feel better. Talking also helps because other people can then let you know that your feelings are normal and natural under the circumstances. Knowing that will help you not to worry about yourself. Talking also helps because sometimes others will be able to help you find a solution to your problem, once you let them know how you feel.

"When considering talking to others, it's important to choose a person whom you trust. Choose someone who cares about you, who you believe is honest, and whom you can count on to be helpful to you."

V.   TRUST-CIRCLES EXERCISE

A.   Ask the children to identify the good qualities that help them trust a person. Make a list of these qualities on the chalkboard or flip chart— honest, caring, helpful, respects confidentiality, fair, and so forth.

B.   Pass out paper and crayons or markers.

C.   Ask the children to think about all the people they trust. Remind them to consider their daily routines, so they can try to remember everyone they have contact with, both family and nonfamily members.

D.   Have the children draw a large circle on their papers. Within that circle, ask them to draw a picture of all the people they trust.

When they have completed that picture, tell them that they may also draw the people they do **not** feel comfortable talking with or confiding in on the outside of the circle. Explain to the children that this may help them choose the people with whom they feel comfortable sharing their thoughts and feelings.

E. Compile a list on the board of all the kinds of people the children identified within their circles (i.e., mother, father, sister, teacher, school nurse, counselor, clergyperson, and so forth).

F. Ask the group if, due to what another child shared, any of them thought of someone who hadn't occurred to them previously. Comment on how many different kinds of people were identified.

Stress to the group that it can be helpful for them to share feelings with people they trust.

VI. MINI-LECTURE: FAMILY MEETINGS

"Another good way to express your feelings to family members and to work out family problems is to have a family meeting. At a family meeting, all family members are called together to talk about common concerns. Each member can share what he or she thinks and all members can try to find solutions to individual or family problems. It's important to establish rules for family meetings, such as the rules we have for the group. Especially important rules are that only one person speaks at a time and everyone gets a turn. If you feel a family meeting might be helpful to you, explain how it works to your mom or dad and ask your parents to set up a time for a meeting."

VII. OPTIONAL EXERCISE

If you asked the children to draw pictures of "three wishes" in Session 2 (section V, p. 19), this session offers a good point at which to repeat that exercise. You can compare the two sets of pictures and what they represent before the next session and share any pertinent findings with the children in a positive, supportive way.

For example, a child's initial picture might display the wish that his parents would reunite. Several sessions and many discussions later the child's second picture might depict him relating to the current family constellation in a more positive way, which would indicate greater acceptance of the reality and permanence of his parents' divorce. Another example might be an initial picture of a magic wand or genie who would put the child's family back together again. If, in a later drawing, the child depicts herself in a fun activity with friends or family, this may indicate that the child has moved toward developing more positive and constructive coping mechanisms to deal with the family breakup.

VIII. SUMMARY OF SESSION

Review for the group the key ideas for this session:

A. Becoming involved in activities we enjoy, such as hobbies or sports, helps us cope with negative feelings.

B. Talking or communicating with people whom we trust is another way of dealing with feelings.

C. Talking to family members in a family meeting about concerns is yet another way of coping with feelings.

IX. ANTICIPATING THE NEXT SESSION

Explain to the children that the following week is the final group session. In that session, group members will continue to talk about
themselves, their beliefs about themselves, and how they feel about
themselves.

Also, the group will talk about making good decisions and review
what they have done for the past eight weeks. They will prepare to
say good-bye to one another as the group comes to an end.

Session 8
BUILDING SELF-ESTEEM

OBJECTIVES

✔ To help children overcome the tendency to blame one parent for the family rupture or split positive and negative attributes between parents.

✔ To enhance the child's self-esteem by identifying and validating positive characteristics in each group member

✔ To reestablish a sense of control in participants' lives through consideration of decision-making opportunities

✔ To review key ideas and suggestions from throughout the group sessions

✔ To provide an opportunity to say good-bye and bring closure to the group

MATERIALS

✔ Paper and pens or pencils for making lists

✔ Evaluation questionnaires for participants and their parents

BRIEF OUTLINE

   I. Opening the Session
  II. Mini-Lecture: Who Are You?
 III. Identity and Self-Esteem Exercise
 IV. Decision Making, Power, and Control Discussion
  V. Review of the Workshop
 VI. Evaluation
VII. Closure

I. OPENING THE SESSION

Ask group members if they have any questions or comments related to last week's discussion. Remind them that this is the last group meeting. In addition to talking about self-esteem and making decisions, everyone will have a chance to say good-bye at the end of the session.

II. MINI-LECTURE: WHO ARE YOU?

"As soon as you were born, your family began talking about whom you resembled in your family. Relatives said things like 'She looks just like her mother!' or 'He has his father's nose!' And you weren't even a week old! Each of us inherits characteristics from our parents. Physically, you might have your mother's eye color and your father's hair. A part of your personality, like your sense of humor, may be similar to one parent, and your aptitude for math may be like the talent of the other parent. Though we all resemble our parents in some or even many ways, each of us is also a brand new combination, both in the way we look and the way we act. Each of us is unique—completely original—a one of a kind!

"People are not 'all good' or 'all bad.' Each of us has strengths and weaknesses. Each of us does some things well, and all of us have parts of ourselves that we need to change or improve. The same is true of our parents. No parent is all good or all bad. No one parent can take the whole blame for a family breaking up. Sometimes, in a divorced family, children make the mistake of blaming everything on just one parent. Because they are feeling hurt and angry in relation to that parent, they feel that that parent is 'all bad.' Things are hardly ever that simple. Like all of us, our parents have positive and good qualities as well as parts of them that need to be changed or improved. Each parent has things to offer us from which we can learn. Sometimes these things are hard to see clearly, especially right after the separation and divorce, when you are feeling really hurt and confused. It takes time to sort out your feelings and begin to see clearly. Let's see if we can talk today about ways to help that process along."

III. IDENTITY AND SELF-ESTEEM

A. Ask the children to write brief lists in response to the following questions.

1. How are you like your mother?
2. What are her positive traits?
3. How are you like your father?
4. What are his positive traits?

B. Ask the children to make a list of things that they like about themselves. Remind them that they should include personal qualities in addition to physical characteristics, for instance, their talents, skills, personality traits, and so forth.

C. To stimulate group discussion, ask some of the children to share several items from their lists with the group. Or, as group leader, share your own list. Use these examples to emphasize the following points:

1. Children are the products of both parents.
2. Each parent has something to offer a child that the child can learn from.
3. Children can choose to imitate each parent's strengths.
4. Each child in the group has many positive characteristics.

As group leader, you may be able to note characteristics you have observed about each child that the child can add to his or her list. Try to elicit input from group members as you do this, because personal compliments that are reinforced by peers carry a lot of weight. Remind group members, before they speak, to think about the pictures and activities that each child has contributed as a way of refreshing their memories and bringing other ideas to mind. Summarize the discussion by reminding them that each one of them is special and has a lot of things about which he or she can be proud.

IV. DECISION MAKING, POWER, AND CONTROL

Tell group members that often, when a family separates, one of the many uncomfortable feelings that family members—especially the children—may have is that of being "out of control." Parents and other adults are making major decisions about the children's lives, and things may be changing at a very fast pace. As a result, the children may feel that they have lost a sense of control over their life.

In the midst of all of this, it is important to think of ways in which you still have control in your life and decisions you still can make. It will be helpful to concentrate your energy on these things, in areas where you can make a difference.

A. Ask group members the following questions. You may want to jot their responses down on a chalkboard or newsprint pad. Or the children may want to make lists of their own answers.

1. What decisions do you make now in your life: Think of your routine each day, each weekend. For example, do you choose the clothes you wear to school? What to eat for breakfast? How to decorate your room? What friends to be with? What to do on visits with your parents?

2. Are there decisions that you currently do not make that you feel you may be ready to handle? Some examples might be staying home alone for short periods, trying a new sport, and learning a new household task such as doing the wash or starting supper. Share some of your ideas with the group.

3. Ask the group to discuss how they can work toward the goal of making these decisions. If group members are stymied, the leader can offer suggestions to help the discussion along. For instance, a child might ask his or her mother or father to

have a family meeting, as discussed in the previous group
session, in order to talk about the idea of new decisions.
Or perhaps another child could suggest a trial plan to test
a new decision, activity, or responsibility with parental
permission.

4. Encourage the children to put these plans into action at
   home if they feel ready to assume more decision-making
   responsibility.

V.   REVIEW OF THE WORKSHOP

A. The process of reviewing the ideas covered in workshop sessions
    can be facilitated by asking the children to compile their draw-
    ings and written exercises into their personal group books. At this
    point, return the materials you have collected to the children. Ask
    them to look over their own productions as you review key ideas
    presented at the group sessions. They can arrange their illustra-
    tions and activity sheets in order as you talk. Then, depending on
    available materials, the leader may ask the children to put their
    drawings and sheets in a folder, bind them with yarn or string, sta-
    ple them together, or create special book covers as an additional
    group activity.

    As you review the main ideas of previous sessions, list important
    points on a chalkboard or on newsprint. If you like, have the chil-
    dren write down the main points themselves to make their own
    lists for inclusion at the end of their books.

B. Older children benefit from an additional review exercise. Ask
    them to incorporate important ideas that they have gotten from
    the group into the format of a newspaper "advice column." An
    example of such a column written by one of our groups is includ-
    ed at the end of this session to illustrate this activity. Ask the chil-
    dren to think of activities or advice that were particularly helpful
    to them in dealing with divorce. After the group has offered their
    own contributions, read the advice column at the end of this ses-

sion. Note that it was written by children in a group similar to theirs, and point out a few ideas that group members missed, or ask if the children want to add additional items to their list. You might add that some groups have submitted their advice lists to school newsletters for publication, sent them to local newspapers for a feature article, or displayed them on church bulletin boards in order to share their ideas with other children. If it is possible to do so, include either the group list of key ideas, a prepared list of important points, or the group "advice column" in the material distributed for the children's personal books.

C. Review activities completed at previous group meetings to emphasize the following key ideas:

1. Families come in many different shapes and sizes. Basically, a family is anyone you live with and anyone you love.
2. Separation and divorce in a family leave children with many different feelings. It is normal to feel many kinds of emotions, some good, some bad, and some that are confusing or mixed.
3. Loss is a part of life for all of us. The changes that divorce brings to a family often mean many losses must be faced and dealt with by both children and parents.
4. Children are not to blame when their parents divorce.
5. Activities you enjoy can help you to cope with problems.
6. It is important to find someone whom you can trust to talk with when something is bothering you.
7. Both of your parents can offer or teach you something positive.
8. Each of you is special. Build on your strengths.
9. Assume responsibility in your life according to your age and ability.

V. EVALUATION

As part of this final session, an evaluation can provide leaders with valuable feedback that will be helpful in planning and conducting future groups. We find it helpful to gather input from parents as well as the children in order to assess the impact that the group has had. Included at the end of this session are sample evaluation forms that can be adapted for your own purposes.

VI. CLOSURE

Allow time at the end of this session for the children to share their feelings about the ending of the group and to say good-byes. It is often helpful for the leader to express his or her feelings first, to set the stage and provide a model for the children to follow.

EVALUATION QUESTIONNAIRE FOR
CHILDREN OF DIVORCE GROUP

Please circle the number that describes your feelings in response to each statement.

Strongly Disagree	*Disagree*	*Neutral*	*Agree*	*Strongly Agree*
1	2	3	4	5

1. The group helped me to talk about divorce.

    1   2   3   4   5

2. I'm glad that I joined the group.

    1   2   3   4   5

3. I'm sorry I joined the group.

    1   2   3   4   5

4. I liked the books we used.

    1   2   3   4   5

5. I liked the skits we did.

    1   2   3   4   5

6. I liked the videos we saw.

    1   2   3   4   5

7. I liked the drawings/exercises we did.

    1   2   3   4   5

8. I liked it when we just talked.

    1   2   3   4   5

9. I think other kids could benefit from a group like this one.

    1   2   3   4   5

10. I would join another group if I could.

    1   2   3   4   5

Please complete the following sentences.

1. This group helped me learn _____
   _____
   _____

2. What I liked most about the group is _____
   _____
   _____

3. What I liked least about the group is _____
   _____
   _____

4. The group helped me to change_____
   _____
   _____

5. I wish the group _____
   _____
   _____

6. The group leader was _____
   _____
   _____

EVALUATION QUESTIONNAIRE FOR PARENTS
OF CHILDREN OF DIVORCE GROUP

What aspect of the group do you think was most helpful to your child?

_____
_____
_____
_____
_____

What aspect of the group do you feel was least helpful to your child?

_____
_____
_____
_____
_____

How could this group have been more helpful to you and your child?

_____
_____
_____
_____
_____

Is your child talking any differently about the situation at home since the workshop began?

_____
_____
_____
_____
_____

ADVICE FROM INVOLVED CHILDREN

Participants in the first two Children of Divorce support groups in Nazareth schools wrote this advice column for other children of divorce.

1. Talk to your teachers. They are not so bad and they understand you.
2. Sometimes crying helps to get out all the anger. After you have cried a lot, realize that crying will not bring your parents back together.
3. Read books about divorce, like "Dinosaurs Divorce" and "The Boys and Girls Book about Divorce."
4. Play video games or any kind of games.
5. Keep busy. Join a sport. Get involved in activities.
6. Take your anger out in sports or on the ball. Do not take the anger out on people or pets.
7. Listen to music.
8. Join a group about coping with divorce.
9. Be good to your friends. You need them. Choose them carefully for they can help you.
10. Avoid people who use you. Do not be a spy for your parents.
11. Do not lie about one parent to the other parent.
12. Try not to feel so down about the divorce.
13. Try to find a friend who will talk to you and will listen. Hopefully they will not just say, "It will be all right," for sometimes it isn't.
14. If you start getting mad, do some kind of activity that wears you out and gets the anger out. A running coach said, "Run out your frustrations."
15. Let your feelings out.
16. Ask your parents for a pet, like a dog, cat, ferret, or elephant.
17. If it bothers you, go see your guidance counselor or a family counselor.
18. Go fishing.

ABOUT THE AUTHORS

MARILYN A. DAVENPORT, ACSW, LSW, is Director of Marketing, Development and Special Services at Family and Counseling Services of the Lehigh Valley in Allentown, Pennsylvania. She earned her undergraduate degree from Pennsylvania State University and attended Boston University School of Social Work for her master's. In addition to her role in planning and promoting agency programs and services, Ms. Davenport has twenty years of clinical experience conducting custody evaluations and providing court systems with programs for divorcing parents.

PATRICIA L. GORDY, ACSW, LSW, is Director of Clinical Services at Family and Counseling Services of the Lehigh Valley. Ms. Gordy received her bachelor's degree from Denison University and her MSW from Boston University School of Social Work. She is an approved supervisor for the American Association of Marriage and Family Therapists. In her extensive clinical work, Ms. Gordy has led children of divorce groups in both agency and school settings.

NANCY A. MIRANDA, ACSW, LSW, received her undergraduate degree from Long Island University and her master's degree in social work from Virginia Commonwealth University. She is Director of the Families in Separate Houses program at Family and Counseling Services of the Lehigh Valley. This program, known by the acronym FISH, provides a variety of services to families, adults, and children who have experienced the breakup of their families.